A Place of

Broken Dreams

by Rick Savage

E&R

PUBLISHERS OF O.G. AUTHOR GENIUSES

Published by E&R Publishers New York
www.EandR.pub

Cataloging-in-Publication information is available from the Library of Congress.

Library of Congress Control Number: 2022943340
ISBN: 9781945674471 (Hardcover)
ISBN: 9781945674723 (Paperback)
ISBN: 9781945674709 (Audiobook)
ISBN: 9781945674716 (Ebook)

First Edition

Dedication

Please take these words
and wrap them around yourself
as if they were a robe woven
of the finest material
and feel their warmth
as they came from my heart
and know full well
that I wish they could be my arms

Ackowledgements

I would like to thank the people who have supported me as a writer for many years. Reading my work and helping to mould me as an artist.

Lisa Claudia Briggs—MSW
Carl Haggerty
Erma Orofino
Patty Ewald FMR Executive Director the Actors Studio
Jimmy Delrossi
James F. Mueller—Author, Confessions of St. Augustine

In memorium
To Dorota Rose Ellington.
My original muse who started me on the path and perhaps is looking down on me as I continue my journey.

About the Work

This book of free-form prose is crafted to let the reader wander through as if it were a park with curved paths, treelined haunted passages, sunny vistas, solid rocky overhangs to sit and ponder, and a liberal dose of pain to help you heal.

TABLE OF CONTENTS

I TASTE LIKE THE DREAMS OF MAD CHILDREN

I taste like the dreams of mad children
I wander in the halls of a thousand abandoned buildings
Left behind from a former time
The bricks still hold the memories of screams
Forgotten by everyone
Except for me
I go looking for the morgue
It is somewhere here the forgotten
Souls come out at night
Why did you leave us here
And never come back
Our cardboard suitcases
So neatly stored
Still there in a room
Our names in white paint
Addresses long gone
In cities and streets
That no longer appear in our books or our phones
These children all left behind in a former time
What was their crime
To be locked away
For no one to see
For no one to be
There for them all left alone
With names that sounded like heaven
A place of beauty and not of despair
All alone with no one to care
I taste like the dreams of mad children
Scrawled on the walls
Endless tile halls
Who placed the last toe tag
Who wrote it in the book
Now thrown on the floor
To be looked at no more lost in time
The pain and the fear still permeates the walls
You can burn down it all
The screams still remain
That belie the pain
I taste like the dreams of mad children
Scream it out to the world
Let everyone know
I taste like the dreams of mad children
Scream it out to the world
Let everyone know

1

That place
In the cauldron of love
Falling back down
The road to the town

A PLACE OF BROKEN DREAMS

A place of broken dreams
Or so it always seems
To be just out of reach They never did teach
You to resign
Yourself to fail or achieve
The things you always saw
On the other side of the sunrise But you may surmise
From the way you dreamed
You never could touch that place In the sky
You never wondered why Neither did I
Or ever try to reach
That place
In the cauldron of love
Falling back down
The road to the town
Well traveled in places
Forget all the faces
You saw along the way
On the side of the road
There were broken dreams Left by those
Who passed through the town Gathered the tears
Spent all the years
Trying to make sense
Of the derelicts Left behind
Shipwrecks and fools
Didn't have the tools
To play by the rules
Picking up the pieces
Of the broken dreams
Left behind
Like paintings of an unknown time before

ALL THE PHOTOS

Once we were real
All these photos
Time passed never to repeat
As we look at the memories
The images perhaps faded Come back to life
Record time spent
People who are no more
Words and memories lost in time
Our fingers run over the faces
Leaving traces in the dust
Of our past
Never meant to last
Fade as time forges on
I want to die all the ways
You can
Live all the lives
I will never see
Take all the photos of places I will never be Long to see
All the friends I will never have
Saved in that album of photos
Never to be opened
But we now have the moments
That we share our children look back
On the endless wars we fought
The faithful and faithless partners
Now lost and forgotten in time
Quaint dress and hair sometimes
Not so sublime
All the photos of all of us lined up in time The tears and the joyous moments
Now written in dust
Our sacred vows
And all of our trust
Just open the book
And take a quick look Transfixed like a butterfly
Or a flower pressed in a book The beauty has faded
The fame has gone South Once we were real
All these photos
Time passed never to repeat

OF WHO YOU MAY FEAR

Of who you may fear
Of what you hold dear
The tide at its ebb
Exposes as it flows
Let your pride go
So all that may know
Just as the tide
Exposes with its flow
How vulnerable you truly are
Just let it go and let it ride
Along with the tide
Yes you shall rise
As one did before
Release your fear
Of all you may hold dear
You are such a pretty one
No one can not see
All you should be
Just let go and you shall rise
Perhaps much to your surprise
The beauty in your eyes
You really are such a pretty one
You have worn the disguise
For far too long
It's time to come home
To be one with your name
You will never complain
Just let it go
No one shall know
Of who you may fear
Of what you hold dear
The ghosts are long gone
They can do you no harm
So just let it go
And give up your fear
Of all you hold dear

ANGEL OF RESURRECTION

Stand over my tomb
And guard me from the future
All my past is gone
My present unchanged
All my love like the shoreline
Of a forgotten sea
Recedes into memory
While your stony countenance
Stares into the void
Are you the angel of my resurrection
Are you my final protection
A heart of stone
Your beauty shown
For all to see
Who remember me
As time forgets all
No tears fall from your face
My mortal coil longed for your embrace
Long before I forgot your face
Now silently in stone
You guard this lonely place
Stand guard and protect me from the future
Be the angel of my resurrection
Be my final protection

Where were his stars
When fate took his legs
Pushing himself
With 2 wooden pegs
On a train in the Bronx

HARMONIUM PANDEMONIUM

The man comes into view
Pushing his cart
In-between cars
Where were his stars
When fate took his legs
Pushing himself
With 2 wooden pegs
On a train in the Bronx
Now lost in time
Only a memory
For a very small child
But what remains
Is the sound of the train
As he took out his weapon of Gabriel
And played out to heaven
In sync with the clicks on the track
I wish I could go back
Just one more time
A sound so sublime
Burned in my psyche
Till the end of time
A chromatic harmonica
Came into view
Playing in two keys
With the noise of the train
I know I witnessed this
Like the savior once did
Who was he and who was I
To hear the notes
As they rose to the sky

I WAS JUST ANOTHER CARDBOARD JESUS

I was just another cardboard Jesus
A savior through and through
Hold the double edge
Make the cut straight and true
All the women you once loved
All the women you once knew
The empty sidewalk
And the cracked concrete
Rises up and bows down
Before your weary feet
I was just another cardboard Jesus
But I didn't know anything about saving
When it came to saving you
Pass me by on the left pass me by on the right
Please be my savior all through the night
I was just another cardboard Jesus
Just another one on the heap
Discarded saviors
Fallen in disgrace
A dime a dozen gathered in this place
Just another cardboard Jesus
With no miracles to perform
Standing on a vacant corner
Washed up and forlorn
Just another cardboard Jesus
A savior through and through
But I didn't know anything about saving
When it came to saving you

OH, HOW I TAMED YOU

My steed who was afraid of his own shadow
I threw my cloak on the ground
Your shadow you could not see
Oh how wild you were
for the cost of 13 talents
how much gold even for a king
A ransom for a son
Kingdoms no longer known
Battles no longer fought
Bravery no longer remembered
Yet down through millennia
Your name still burns inside
Bucephalus a beautiful black horse
Your name still resounds as one
Untameable
Yet you came to me
You did not know I was a king
Or a warrior
Or would conquer half the world
Nor could I be tamed
and my epithet was
Sic Transit Gloria Mundi
Even my father did not know
But you Bucephalus you were my constant
Ran with me in battle
Beneath me
Your strength
Your beauty
The Oracle told your father
that he who would ride you
Would become king of the world
The horse with the mark of the ox on his haunch
You died in battle and laid to rest
In the city of your death
No longer to be ridden
no sleek black coat to stroke
Bucephalus a name worthy of a kingdom

I get up once more Fight one more round
In the ring of love
Caught a right
In the jaw

GET UP OFF THE FLOOR

Every time each and every time
I get knocked down
My heart wounded The bell sounded In the ring of love
Someone has a weight in their glove
Knocked me out
I get up once more Fight one more round
In the ring of love
Caught a right
In the jaw
Didn't think
I would live to love another night
In the ring of love
The fight is fixed
Before you even climb the rope Just give up hope
But each and every time I get up once more
To fight one more round In the ring of love
I kiss the ground
A whimper my only sound
I get up one more time
To fight one more round

Let's cry together
Drown in all of our tears

BEYOND LOVE

What's beyond love
Fits like a glove
Let's cry together
Drown in all of our tears
All of the years that have passed between All of the moments
Or so it does seem
Is there a description Of what we have seen Who is watching
As we go marching To our celebration Will there be libation Our thirst
quenched
In tears we are drenched Ones of joy or sorrow There is no way to know
The map of our emotions erased Our steps cannot be retraced Written in the
clouds
You held someone's hand That you loved in totality They could die knowing
They were loved till the end of time Please let me know that you are mine
Never to own but to shine
In my universe
As a star so bright Behold the light
The love shines from within Now we begin
To build the temple
Where love is worshipped
But never defiled
Show me the path That we must follow
One step before the next
Perhaps we had met sometime before
It is difficult to ignore
The signs were always there What's beyond love

Come into my life
With your sadness
Drown in your remorse

COME INTO MY LIFE

Come into my life
With your sadness
Drown in your remorse
What are the condiments
You slather on of course
Tears on tears
Flow through the years
Make the call
To end it all
I thought I would never
See you again
Loneliness brings your
Parcel to my door
Who were you?
So long ago
I didn't think I would
Know you anymore
Of course, you always
Showed up like before
Each time a little more worn
A life more torn and forlorn
In your book of time
Passes without any respite
No matter who tried
To hold you through the night
I guess one more last time
Before we say goodbye

How far did we fall
From that lofty place
Was it then that
We fell from grace

GRACE

I'm moved by your beauty
I'm moved by your grace
I hide behind the lines
I read on your face
I cannot believe
All the years gone by
There never was love
As much as we tried
I stare into the well
Of your deep green eyes
There was no bottom
Much to my surprise
Did we really meet
When we were so young
You took the love
From the tip of my tongue
How far did we fall
From that lofty place
Was it then that
We fell from grace
All the other souls
We inflamed since then
Were sacrifices
On the altar of love
Just one flower in the garden
That never died
I tried to forget you
As hard as I tried
A comet that comes
Once a millennium
And lights up the skies
Many are fearful
And shield their eyes
We were never afraid
Of the flames so high
I will never forget you
Till the day that I die

**What tidal force
As the moon pulls on the Earth
Will finally bring us together**

PATHS

Was it you that walked in my footsteps
Left on the station floor
As I walk down the stairs
I know our hands have touched the same place on the railing
Many times before
The very same way our footsteps
Have merged on the floor
Unbeknownst to either of us
From some time before
Was it you I saw from the window
Of the passing train
On the platform
Standing in the rain
Your hair, a storm unto itself
I remember your face
From some unknown time and place
Burned in my psyche
I knew one day we would meet
From the path, our feet took
Left on the street
was it you that crossed my path
On the station floor
I felt your presence then
And knew I wanted more
What tidal force
As the moon pulls on the Earth
Will finally bring us together
That question still remains
As I sit here and wonder
As to who is guiding the cart
And in whose hands
Are the reins

EVERY WHORE HAS A NAME

Every whore has a name
They hide from everyone
It buries the pain
In the past they no longer want to see
While walking the stroll life taking its toll on thee
Blessed be the children and the women of the night
Who judges them, what is their right?
Painted face, fallen from grace
Who are the men who walk with you in disgrace
How did you fall
Tell it to all who may care
Wipe up your tears, gather your fears
Walk one more day
Put on your face that shows no disgrace
Only a smile for all that would stop
And spend a moment in your embrace
Loving like only you know how
Hold these broken souls
Close to yours
Every whore has a name
They show to none
Under the sun
But only let it out
In their dreams
To someone who would fall in love
As if they were not in the life
But that is a dream
Or so it may seem
Keep looking for the one
But every whore has a name
They share with no one

HARK THE HERALD ANGELS

Behind St.Patricks church 51st street Madison Avenue

Hark the herald Angel's sing
Old lady sitting in the cold
Nighttime in New York
Glory to the newborn king
All the feet walking by
No one to even look or cry
Peace on earth, and mercy mild
What brought her here
She was once a child
As beautiful as the one
Hark the herald Angel's sing
Glory to the newborn king
Ambulance lights flashing
The giant tree all ablaze in color
The old lady silent night
Lay me down to rest
Hark the herald Angel's sing
Glory to the newborn king
All the feet passing by
Wrapped in rags
When she has died
Hark the herald Angel's sing
Glory to the newborn king
Did anyone else look and care
Anyone else stop and stare
Who was she once a child
What brought her here
Hark the herald Angel's sing
Glory to the newborn king
Behind a church voices inside
Sing in praise of a savior outside
Wrapped in rags
Perhaps she is the newborn king
Hark the herald Angel's sing
Glory to the newborn king

JUKE BOX QUARTER

Where did you get the stain?
Pink nail polish
What was your game
Place your quarter in the slot
Feed the music
Join me for the last dance
Hold me tight and take a chance
A jukebox quarter
One free ride
Just one dance
Swallow your pride
And take your ride
Look at my face and in my eyes
Hold me tight Just once more this night
Hear this song
And this dance
A marked quarter Is your last chance
Flip it now, heads or tails
Your life is marked just like a jukebox quarter
Place it in the slot and begin the slaughter
There is no time not to take a chance
Will you join me in this very last dance
You're marked just like a jukebox quarter
Where did you get the stain
Forever will remain
There is no time not to take a chance
Will you join me in this very last dance

Shall I set a place
Where you used to sit
And pass the time
Watching you as you ate
The meal now on the empty plate

CONVERSATIONS WITH THE DEAD

Now that you're gone
I can tell you all the things
I should have said
Now that you're gone
I can read to you from all the books
We should have read
Now that you're gone
I can only shake my head
When you do not answer
All your words left unsaid
Our time in this time
Is like no time before
Our time next time is nevermore
So many words left unsaid
So many books left unread
Conversations now with the dead I cook a meal
Now only for one
Shall I set a place
Where you used to sit
And pass the time
Watching you as you ate
The meal now on the empty plate
I find a strand of your hair
Left upon the pillow on our bed
Now it's up to me
To have a conversation with the dead
I put my foot in the river where we once stood
Knowing full well
That very same river is gone for good
And even I am not the same man
When I held you close
Between our legs that water ran

Our lives now years apart
The distance an ocean
Beyond any horizon

I DREAMED

I dreamed I made love to you
As if we truly cared
Held your face
With both my hands
Saw the desire within your eyes
No, it was never there
I slowly drew you close
Your eyes now closed
Only the feeling
Of being connected
Now posed
But when I awoke
The dream curled up like smoke
Of times we never had
Leaving me so sad
If only life had been like the dream
It would have been so easy
Or so it seemed
To have combined
Two as one
The feeling now undone
Could it ever have been
As if in the dream
No, it does not seem
As if floating on that cloud
Would ever have been allowed
Our lives now years apart
The distance an ocean
Beyond any horizon
The deep passion seen fit
The love to remit
Was just not there
But only in a dream

I bleed for vision
The pain of the incision
Who makes the decision
Who bleeds for us all

I BLEED

I bleed for the trees
Makes me want to get down on my knees
In some crazed technicolor dream
I want to try but I don't see all the words
Left unsaid
Shall I let you complete
My thoughts my words my deeds
Unknown memories
How could you ever know
You were never shown the path
Or so we thought
Perhaps all for naught
You cannot perceive
Or, for that matter, believe
What you were never told
It is not for me to
Be the one on the other side
We can all deride
Where none can hide
I bleed for love
Someone below or
One never knows
How to end the thought
I bleed for the lame
Nothing for me to gain
I bleed for the frail
To no avail
I bleed for all the fools
For no one has taught us the rules
I bleed for vision
The pain of the incision
Who makes the decision
Who bleeds for us all
The mighty stand tall
So they may fall
On deaf ears
The words I may speak
I bleed for them all

Hardly a moment goes by
If only I
Could reach through time

I CAN SEE IN YOUR YARD

Sometimes I can see in your yard
Your life has been so hard
Hardly a moment goes by
If only I
Could reach through time
I tried
To ease the pain
It all comes back again
So turn
Turn your face to the sky
Let the rain become your tears
Wash away all your fears
The last time I saw you
You took my hand
And pressed it to my heart
You said keep me here
Till the end of time
I said we will never part Sometimes
I can see in your yard
Your life has been so hard
Hardly a moment goes by
If only I
Could reach through time
I tried
To ease the pain
One day
We will meet again

Never looking back
At the dead and dying
You left behind

ONE DAY YOU WILL TELL YOUR STORY

One day you will tell your story
People will bow their heads
Solace remains in glory
Perhaps there was a moment in time
When you made the choice
To cross the line
Never looking back
At the dead and dying
You left behind
All your thoughts
Now memories
Fade away as the curtain draws closed
No one will ever know
The truth
Or the last act
Of the show
The faded ink on the newspaper
Blows down the street
Curls up and lays by your feet
Like a stray dog ignored
No hand to stroke the fur
Love never lasts just like that cur
Looking up with begging eyes
The headline now in the past
Signifies your desire to last
More than your allotted time
Not that you know your place in line
No one ever really does
Anyone really care
Spend the time to stop and stare
At the hands on the clock
Stop time in its track
And never look back

PIECES OF THE PUZZLE

You were so broken
No one had spoken
The lines
I crossed late at night
Walked across to the other side
Where no one goes
And no one knows
Your name
I tried to pick up the pieces
The quilt woven tight
Soaked in blood
And strife
Put together the puzzle
Of your life
No one gave a damn
Who you were
You said I could take you
Like every other man did
You slid out of your clothes
Before I changed my mind
Rolled in sweat and remorse
Before I changed the course
You even said your name
Before we came
To the point of no return
I tried to pick up the pieces
No one can release
Your soul
Before someone
picks up the pieces
And tries to put the puzzle
Back into one

As our friends pass through this world
We are all lost as the fool
Or perhaps
The Truth

THE FOOL

Like a fool in a snowstorm
Standing on the street corner
Face to the sky
Trying to catch the snowflakes on his tongue
Below the still waters, the bivalves pump as they always have for eons
Filtering out the nutrients
The snowflakes silently form a blanket on the river
Gone all too soon unknown to anyone
I stand all alone in the middle of the crowd quiet approaches this singular
death I notice
No one cries
The fool still standing on the corner now selling his soul for love
No one has told him yet the river runs deep as his love
We do not want nor care for the truth
As it comes from the tongue of a fool
All of us
Lost in our own thoughts
Blinded by the glare of the sun
Quiet in our quest for someone
To tell us the lies we all desire
The currents of the river
Flowing to the sea
We ignore
As we always do the important
Or so we think
The fool stands firm
Solid is the stance
Never wavers
As our friends pass through this world
We are all lost as the fool
Or perhaps
The Truth

The bricks and stones now lay as the
Bodies once did
Buried in time

A FIELD OF BROKEN STONES

A field of broken stones lay out before me
As far as the eye can see
Each one a memory erased
Of a time before debased
The memories of what came before
Hidden with each stone as they
Lay upon the floor
Many fields
Many nations
The waving fields of grass
Cover the stones
As they recced in time
Each one a story
Reassemble the broken stones
Reassemble the shattered bones
They were people once before
Now lost in time
Their stories never more
To be told
Every drop of blood
Upon this hallowed ground
Fell like tear drops
Silently without a sound
There are those
Who hide behind the past
There are those
Whose silence
Belie their steadfast
Refusal to accept the truth
But the memories stay with the youth
Whose strength saved them
From the grim fate of the others
Who souls lay within the fields
Never to reveal the awful truth
The bricks and stones now lay as the
Bodies once did
Buried in time

Your inner being wells up
And illuminates your face

BEAUTY WITHIN

Your beauty shines from within
A beacon spreading the light
A glimpse of your soul
Through the crack glowing bright
With the power of a thousand suns
Your inner being wells up
And illuminates your face
There is no mistaking
Your being in grace
I can see through your eyes
The beauty within
The words from your mouth reveal
As the hunger of the doorway
Which all we shall pass through
As your lips unseal
The beauty from within
Make no mistake
And know what is deep inside
Paints on your face
From which nothing can hide
Your heart beating strong
Connects to your hand
And even your fingers follow the command
And through them the beauty must flow
And create a loving glow
For all to know
The beauty from within

**We sit in the cafe
reading the space
In between lives**

BOOK OF LIES

I read from the book
The book of lies
The book of I don't know whys
Hold the book close
So no one may see
Hold it closer for no one to be
Caught up in the lies
To no ones surprise
We all carry this book
But no one may look
At each others book
We sit in the cafe
reading the space
In between lives
No one survives
The scrutiny of what we may see
Open your book
So we may all take a look
At the lies we need to save ourselves
From the turmoil within
No one is kin
To anything we may ask
Of this world we all live in
Throw away the book
and open your eyes
There is no disguise you may wear
You've carried the book so close and so long
It may seem
It has become you
The book of lies
Of I don't know whys
The time has come
To discard all that is past
Now to make it last
Burn the book of lies
Of I don't know whys.

CAN WE

Can we choose
The day we die
How many times
Can we pick
The time to try
How many times
Are written in the book
Have you taken the time
To look
How many times
Have you seen me cry
There must be a reason
I wonder why
Can we choose between
Whom we will love
How many times
Will we see the light
How many times
Have you called out my name
How many times
Has it been in vain
Can we choose
To win or lose
Can we make the time
To draw the line
Can we

Come into my sorrow
And spend the night
Don't forget to hold me tight

COME INTO MY SORROW

Come into my sorrow
The sunrise tomorrow
Illuminates the rocky shore
Tossed onto breaking waves
Overwhelmed with grief
And as always relief
Not to be had
In the half-lit world
Of pain
It all comes back again
In my dreams
Blood red skies
Assault the eyes
That pierce the vail
To no avail
You had no key
To unlock the door
The pain remains evermore
Come into my sorrow
And spend the night
Don't forget to hold me tight
Lest we both slip away
Before the night
Turns into day
Come into my sorrow
And wash my body
In your tears
Don't let the crowd
Haunt you with their jeers
No one can really see you
As you hide behind your fears
Come into my sorrow
Just once more
Before you close
The final door

CRY ME A STORY

Cry me a story
All of the glory
Seen through eyes of pain
There is no surprise
You may surmise
You even forgot your name
There was nothing to gain
From holding on
To the sinking ship
A slip of the lip
Was all it took
To remind you of the story
All of the glory
That passed you by
Written in words in the sky
You may ask me why
I have no answer to this lie
So cry me a story
One of remorse
All of the pain of course
Just let it go
The river will overflow
With your tears on the shore
Everyone will know
Your life with its flow
Drowned in the past
Nothing will last
Your story one of remorse
No never to alter its course
Lift you head up high
Turn your face to the sky
Never ask why
So cry me a story
All of the glory
Seen through your eyes
There is no surprise
Cry me a story

DAY INTO NIGHT

When day turns into night
Some prepare for flight
Knowing that the darkness
Brings with it the fright
Of the unseen
Of the in between
Others delight in the warmth
Of the dark
Illicit walks in the park
Deep in green
Left unseen
Lips meet
Never discreet
When day turns into night
A new morning slowly
Comes into sight
The day and the night
Two sides of the realm
One of dreams
And one of the fight
Attempting to hold back the night
Simple pleasure delight
The demons of the dark and the night
The love spills its right
On the blanket of the night
Quietly the day comes back it seems
In between the dreams

DIE IN YOUR ARMS

Will you deceive me
Will you receive me
I want to die in your arms
There is no time
Like the last time
We met
So much more not to say
Either way
We almost stayed the night
Will you deceive me
Will you receive me
I want to die in your arms
Your lips on mine
There is no time
Like the last time we met
Almost cried
Almost tried
To make it last
Will you deceive me
Will you receive me
I want to die in your arms

Send me a note written in blood
I'll make good on the loan
I'll sign on the line

DO OVER

I petitioned the lord for some do over time
Haven't heard back
But I'm still waiting in line
Send me a note written in blood
I'll make good on the loan
I'll sign on the line
Didn't think it was you who was writing this book
Didn't even take time to read it
Or take a look
Everyone has something that gets away
Everyone has someone that leads them astray
Oh Lord grant me this wish
I promise to be good
Well as good as can be
Just don't hold me to your standard
For I didn't think I could see
The fine writing between the lines
As absolute as could be
Just one more chance
A chance to be me
As imperfect as the last time
A chance to be me

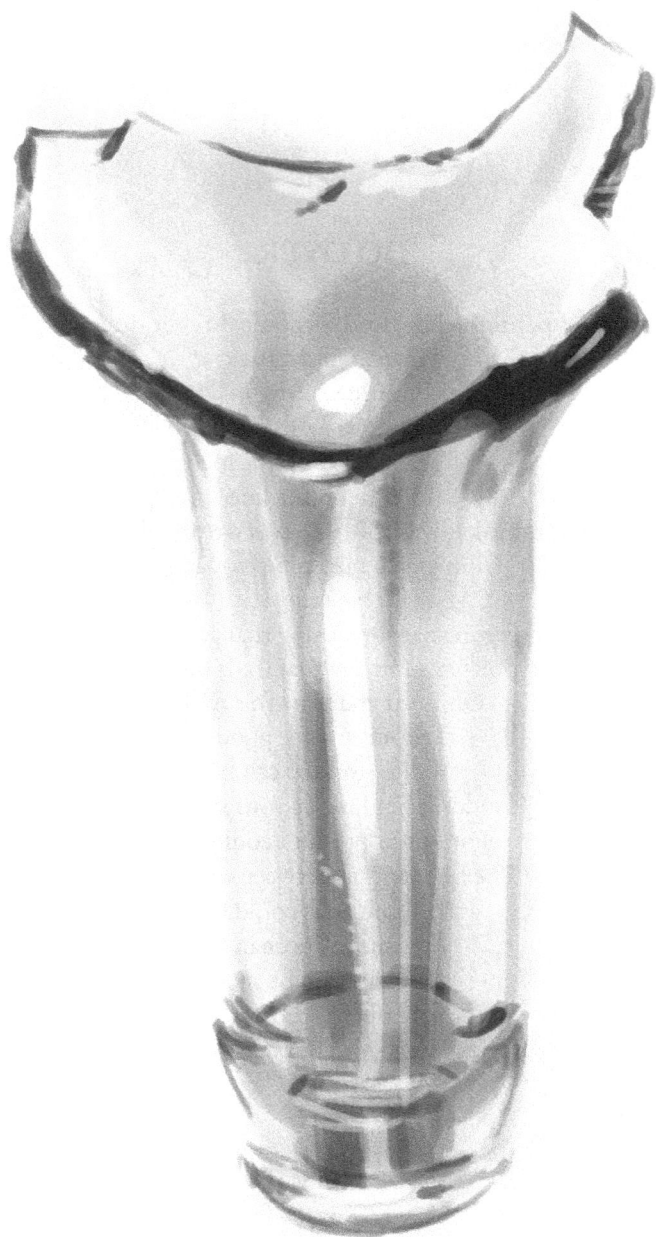

EYES OF THE PAST

Look at it with your eyes of the past
What is it about love
That makes it last
An old bottle of wine
Now lies broken in the grass
Who can tell of the love
That it served once in the past
All of these things we once held dear
Are now discarded
Except for the joy they once brought
Now memories lost in time
Your love and your life now intertwined
The physical no that does not last
And yes it resides in the past
But the love and the joy that it brought
Burns bright as a thousand suns
And no longer resides in our temporal world
But lives on in our spirit
And shines in our memory
Of those moments of joy
Like the broken bottle
Of a solemn vow
That was taken so long ago
When love was so young
We thought it would forever last
Now like the bottle
Lies shattered in the past

GYPSY GIRL TELL ME MY FORTUNE

Gypsy girl tell me my fortune
Tell me what I want to hear
Look in your Crystal Ball
What is it that I fear
Throw the Tarot
Why do you look away
What do the cards say that make you feel this way
What do you know about my life
What do you know about my strife
Pick up your head
Let me look in your deep dark eyes
I'll tell you the future
Much to your surprise
Tell me what you want to hear
Tell me of our journey
That we met up so near
Tell me of your desires
And what is that you fear
Let me hold you in my arms
Let me fold you in my qualms
Your heart is the Tarot
Let's throw it to the evermore
The waves that come crashing into our lives
Send us on our knees to the floor
The holy water cleanses
Our minds and souls of what came before
Let me look in your deep dark eyes
I'll tell you the future
Much to your surprise

HIGH AND MIGHTY

Lonely are you the last one
Spread your arms no longer in need
Wave after wave washed over you
now they no longer come
not at your frequency
Nor at one you even understand
Once you were a crucifix
All roads led to you
Every night you led a chorus
Oh the joy and sorrow you spread
And when you came in all your glory
Mounted atop every monument and building
Screaming out in your glory moment
I will always be here you said
Now you are gone
Left to rust
Huddled in some remote corner
sheltered in a garret forgotten
I went looking for you today
How soon we forget
I saw your proud progeny
At an angle forlorn as if in prayer
No longer of any use
To anyone certainly not me
I wanted to shed a tear
But I didn't there was no need
Yes once you stood so proud and tall
But like all you were doomed to fall
Left lying in rust
In god we trust
You stood aloof your arms outstretched
As if in prayer
Good night good night good night to all

I MET A MAN WHO LOST HIS FAITH

I met a man who lost his faith
I kneeled beside him and told him it was not lost but just misplaced
We held each other in a warm embrace
And looked all over for his faith misplaced
It was not under the pew
Nor behind the altar
Not under the knave nor behind the confessional
Where oh where had his faith ran away
Where oh where had his quest gone astray
The statue of the savior looked down in dismay
As we kneeled in the pews that cold December day
What an odd set of companions a Jew and a priest
Looking for faith in a long abandoned place
No parishioners to kneel for the host
No one left to pray for the most '
No one to bend open the book
Not any one to even take a look
In this once joyous place
Now empty of face
We continued to look for the faith he had misplaced
We looked behind the statue of Mary
And continued to look behind all the saints
Until we came to the patron
And behind Casimir we thought we saw a light
Perhaps it was his faith hiding in the night
We reached out to grab it
But it was elusive and slipped away as if it was in fright
So we continued to look for the faith he had misplaced
How can something so strong disappear without a trace
So I said lets kneel once more
And perhaps it will come back through your knees touching the floor
So we continued to pray all through the night a jew and a priest
Oh what a sight
And once again the sun rose in the East
It bathed the stations
In the morning light
And there was his faith
Hiding in plain sight

71

We both fell in love
Before the night was through

I NEVER KISSED ANYONE SO HARD

I never kissed anyone so hard
As I kissed you
I never held anyone so tight
As I held you
I never knew what hit me
The night that we met
We both fell in love
Before the night was through
Even after all these years
I can still smell your perfume
Wafting through the night
I can still hear your voice
As if you were still beside me
I still see your face in my memory
As if it was a guiding light
I remember 100 people
In some trendy New York bar
Stopped in their tracks
To watch us as we kissed without a care
The world around us disappeared
How could I ever forget that passion?
I remember every curve of your body
As we lay in bed
So many years have passed
Since we let that passion flow
So many years since we let that passion go
Where have you disappeared
That I will never know
I will always remember the kisses
As we bathed in that glow

I SAW A PHOTO

I saw a photo
Of a girl
I used to know
We turned a corner
So long ago
I used to live
Within that dream
All the time that passed
It did seem
Evaporated as if in a flash
As I held that photo
In my hands
My eyes were closed
But I did see
The love that existed
Came back to me
I held it tighter
And the emotions came
Flooding back
As if that piece of paper
Held all that passed
I could not let go
Or let my emotions show
I clenched my jaw
And then I saw
All the lies
I told myself
At that moment in time
Hidden within
That photo I held
I saw a photo
Of a girl I used to know
We turned a corner
So long ago

Sometimes wisdom comes from the fool
They do not understand
The power to rule

I TALK TO CRAZY PEOPLE

I talk to crazy people
Sometimes they make more sense
They can see through the lies
That hide behind the eyes
Of those we say are sane
A pile of pennies by their feet
Each one heaven sent
Never to be spent
A collection of lies
That never made sense
Their life an unmade bed
They have no pretense
Sometimes wisdom comes from the fool
They do not understand
The power to rule
Is it the rein the rain or the reign
It makes no difference
The spectacle is all the same
So stop just one moment
To stare and howl at the moon
Just keep your eyes on the cow
I think you understand now
So you may think you know what truth is
I beg to disagree
No one gave you a lamp to hold up so that you could see
The difference between you and me

I TOUCH THE PLACE

I touch the place my father once touched
I let my hand linger on the place
His rough hand once held
When I looked up I thought I saw his face
Fading away in this mortal place
I touched the place my father once did
I tried to hold onto his hand
As the time passed
Like the sand in the glass
I felt the roughness of his beard
As he kissed me goodnight
One last time
I touched the place my father once did
Held onto a moment
Somewhere in the past
I heard his voice
One last time
As I held onto
The very same place his hand
Once touched
Me close to his heart
Beat felt between the two of us
I tried to make the moment last
As I touched the place he once held
In his heart
Near to him and dear to me
I closed my eyes and held the place he touched
Lest it slip away
As I tried to make it stay
His hand upon mine
I held his hand as we touched the same
Place that he once touched
At the very same time.

Your voice as pure as snow
All young and handsome
Your hair a blonde storm

I WANT TO REMEMBER YOU

I want to remember you
The way you were
All young and handsome
Your hair a blonde storm
I never thought I would ever see you again
I wish I had not
Turned the corner
That moment
I saw you once more
Sitting on the bench
Your face held in your hands
No Jesus or savior
To lift your face to the sky
You could have been famous
Or at least that is what we all thought
You had it in you
How life can change in a second
I want to remember you just the way you were
Like an old movie
Your voice as pure as snow
All young and handsome
Your hair a blonde storm
It was so sad to see you
Down on your luck
I wished I could do anything
Just to pick you up
Life is unfair
To all that would care
I never thought it would all end this way
A story unravels in the day to day
I close my eyes and see you
In all your glory that day
All young and handsome
Your spirit just flew away

**Love doesn't come
Just because you dream**

I WANT TO THANK YOU

I want to thank you
For all the pain
You had nothing to gain
To teach me all the rules
Only fools
Could not see
The vastness of the ocean
Spread out before me
Like a lonely ship
On the sea
Who was I to expect more
So far from the shore
Love doesn't come
Just because you dream
I want to thank you
For all the pain
You had nothing to gain
From seeing me fall
In love once again
All the moments
Washed in time
Each one saying thank you
Dreaming you were mine
My emotions washed away
In tears
I spent all those years
Living on hope
Till I was at the end of my rope
I want to thank you for all the pain
You had nothing to gain
Taught me how to live
Once again

**If my grandmother had wheels
She would be a trolley**

IF

If gives you a way out
If allows you to shout
If is the ultimate excuse
If only I was not a recluse
If my grandmother had wheels
She would be a trolley
If only we could see the folly
If lets you get away
If only you didn't have to pay
What a poor excuse
To let this word loose
If only I had a heart
If only I was smart
If only we could see
If only we could be
If only we could know
If only we could show
Let the Love and compassion flow
If only

No matter the distance
That we walked alone
You were always by my side
As I was by yours

IN ANOTHER TIME

In another time
In another universe
We would have met
When we were young
We had no idea
Who we were
We could not see any further
Than our eyes could tell
The truth always matters
To all the saints and sinners
We met along the way
No matter the distance
That we walked alone
You were always by my side
As I was by yours
Walk in lockstep
But always alone
The vibrations of the Universe
Always rang loud
In our ears
Erase all the fears
And all the tears
Shed along the way
In another time
In another universe
We would have met
When we were young
The time has come
To pull aside the curtain
Of this I am certain
Turn back the clock
And never look back
In another time
We would have met
When we were young

WALTER ROSENSPIRE
PVT 6 MG. BN USMC 2018
N. YORK JUNE 9 1918

87

KIA

Killed In Action

The day started as many before
Bright and sunny
Awake for the last time
How were you to know
Which way to go
One wrong turn
One misstep
Hands on the trigger
The belt fed from the can
A tiny bead of sweat
Forms on your brow
Walter someone
Calls your name
Gas on goes your mask
The green cloud
Another world
In your view
You never heard the shell
Quiet is the blast
Now all lives in the past
No time for tears
No time for fears
The life force
Drains away
The sun still shines
As it will forever
Now in Aisne Marne
Rest forever
In our hearts
Forgotten never

Walter Rosenspire Private unit 6th USMC Machine gun battalion 2nd division
KIA June 9 1918 battle of Belleau Woods Aisne - Marne Cemetery
Plot A Row 2 Grave 87

The last face you will see
I want it to be your face
My last memory

LAST TIME

Even if it's just to say goodbye
I don't need to know the reason why
In this life there's a last time for everything
The last time I held you tight
The last time I kissed you goodnight
Just wander off in my time
Turn a corner
For the very last time
I just guess our love was not so sublime
Just wander off in my time
Turn the corner leave it all behind
There's a last time for everything
That little smile you gave me
Left me on the floor
I guess I won't be seeing that anymore
There's a last call
To end it all
Even if it's just to say goodbye
Don't need to know the reason why
There's a last time for everything
The last breath you take
The last face you will see
I want it to be your face
My last memory
Will never erase
The feelings I had for you
There's a last time for everything
Even if it's just to say goodbye

91

Let me teach you how to cry once more
And water the drought parched land

LET ME TEACH YOU HOW TO CRY

Let me teach you how to cry
On my shoulder
When you left
There were no tears
To get you bye
All of the wonder
Like the images formed
By the clouds moving across the sky
Let me show you the truth
Of the newly mown grass
Like the words of remorse
That grow within
And through your veins course
Silently bringing the tears to your eyes
Let me teach you how to cry once more
And water the drought parched land
On your face
Spring to life the salty river
That needs to flow into your life
Begin the streams that flow into the torrents
From the valleys to the oceans
There is no way to stop
Once the flow begins
Only to end
When the drought
Comes once again
Let me teach you how to cry
Let me look within your eye
Gaze into the past
Lean on my shoulder
And let the river flow

**Like a woman
Watering the Earth
With her tears**

LIKE A WOMAN

Like a woman
Giving birth
To a newborn
Like a woman
Tending flowers
In a garden
Please stand
Next to me
Let me bathe
In your glow
All the things
You say
That I will
Never know
Like a woman
Sitting patiently
To watch the sun
Go down
I drink from
Your wisdom
And vision
You give so freely
As you remove
Your crown
Like a woman
Watering the Earth
With her tears
As we go hurtling
Through the years
Please stand beside me
As I bathe in my fears
Like a woman
Enigma to any man
But with understanding
Wherever you may stand

MISS MEW

Soft was the fur
Gentle was the purr
A tiny package of love
Came into your life
Admits the strife
Reminded you of all the good
For which it stood
But gone all too soon
From this heartless world
She left a gift that will forever be
Buried within your heart
A piece of you when you close your eyes
She will come back to comfort you
Much to your surprise
Never forget the good of those you loved
Now bound to your spirit
Never lost in time
To be cherished
A soft and gentle spirit
Forever to be thine

MOMENTS IN TIME

All these moments
Some well spent
Others wasted
Each infinitesimal slot
Every turn
You make
Brings you here
At the crossroads
Every moment
In your life
Reveals who you have been
And who you will be
Each and every footstep
One before and one after
Brings you to this moment
You light the lamp
Or the cigarette
One man stands before
And one behind
Some will notice
Others pay no mind
Take only one moment
Just stop and look around
Quietly make no sound
Merge with the infinite
Stop to pick up the penny
Laying on the ground
Your connection in time
Makes note of what you found
All those moments between the first and the last
Remain uncounted
And reside in the past
Even memories will not last
Time an endless cycle
Though you cannot see
Reveals to the universe
All that will be
Both in the past and future
And all you currently can see
As Krishna revealed to Arjuna
What was and what will be

MY ARMS

My arms tell you a story
All of the glory
All of the pain
Written on my arms
Not the ones that once held you
In my arms
Which story
Shall I tell you
No need for a voice
Only my choice
What shall I hide
Though you cannot see
Through me to me
An eternal stain
My story will remain
One day to be told
My arms want to hold
You near me to endear me
To contain
All the while to remain
In love forever
Forget the pain
My arms tell you a story
My lips sealed
To never reveal with words
What I never want to say
I prefer to leave it that way
Wrap your arms around me
Tell me a story
Let me close my eyes
And drown in your strength
Rewrite my story
In the ink of glory
A new beginning
Not the end of the story

My God knows all like the drunk in a bar
My God can even drive a car

MY GOD

My God is holier than yours
My God is holier-than-thou
So very holy I worship a Cow
My God is stronger than yours
My God can sort all the straws
Find the needle within at the drop of a pin
My God knows all like the drunk in a bar
My God can even drive a car
Without rubber tires you know who we are
My God is really swell
Forget to praise him and you will roast in hell
My God has been worshiped longer than yours
Let's forget the sacrifices and all the other flaws
My God won't let you eat pork
Don't try to cheat him by using a fork
My God is the true one and I can prove it to you
We have sacred stones that afford quite a view
My God knows where you have been
And will punish you for the sin
You didn't even know where to begin
My God rides the chariot of the Sun
Nobody knows where he goes when the day is done
My God is three into one
Try explaining that to anyone
My God is as confused as you or me
My God will invite you for tea
It all depends on whether you make amends
In which case he will roast you on a spit till time ends
My God is humble, humble as can be
He also controls the sea
In which case he will drown you if you don't leave a sacrifice to thee
My god is a bit crass
He tells you use an odd number of times to wipe your ass
My God oh my God, which one to choose
Seems like no matter what, you'll lose

**Only a fool
Takes the path
That leads one astray**

MY WORDS HOLLOW RING

My words hollow ring
The bell clapper gone
Are the days
That went before
We saw the storm
On the horizon
Bad tidings bring
Us all to a time
In our lives
Where the road
Makes a fork
Only a fool
Takes the path
That leads one astray
From the righteous
Path there is no way
One can choose
The way to go
Shatter your clay gods
At your feet
One day you will
See the truth
Of the words
Hollow ring
Fall from my lips

Have you ever been naked
Covered in clothes

NAKED AND AFRAID

Have you ever been naked
Covered in clothes
Nowhere to hide
Every one knows
There are those who can see within
Carefully count the sin
You thought you could hide
Covered in Pride
But naked inside
Run as fast as you can
From the eyes
That decide
To uncover the truth
You thought your covering could hide
But to tell the truth
We are all naked inside
Naked and scared
No one has dared
To expose the lies
We all hide behind
You can build a brick wall
I guarantee it will fall
You can wear a suit of armor
But in the end
You are naked and scared
No one has cared
To show us the way
To be naked in our life
To maintain it in strife
To show it all to the world
Our nakedness in life

One day this will all fade away
The good and the bad

ONE DAY THIS WILL ALL FADE AWAY

One day this will all fade away
The good and the bad
All the same
One day just one slip away
From finding the truth
There is no reason
For all this to be
There is no corner to turn
Where you can learn
I am glad I was not there to see you fall
I wish to hell I was there to catch you
In my arms
Hold you close
As I once did
Such a short time
You were only mine
I will remember you
Till the end of time
Your name and face
Burned into my heart
Flame forever mine
I can still hear your voice
Echoing through time
Feel you lips
Seared onto mine
There is no reason
For me to forget
There is no season
For my regret
I can't even say I'll be there
Next time
There is no moment
For that to be

ONE DAY WHEN I DIED

One day when I died
I saw a blue light in my hand
Did you see the same
Blue light in your hand
One day when I died
I saw a blue light in my hand
I will never know what you saw
I sit here, the tears stream down my face
I will never know what you saw
One day when I died
I saw a blue light in my hand
I reached out
For all those faces I saw
So near yet so far
In the endless field
Unknown time and tears washed away
I stood in grace
I didn't know it then
I saw your face in the distance
Time stood still
We had not met
Before that time
One day when I died
I saw a blue light in my hand
I will never know what you saw
I sit here, the music plays
As it always has before
The tears stream down my face
Caught out of place
I dream of you as once before
Reach out to touch your face nevermore
One day just one day
Will you see the blue light in your hand
Perhaps then you will understand
As we stand on the hill
In the distance time stood still
One day we saw a blue light in our hands

24- The man turns to look behind realizes it is the last time
25- Somewhere in the universe

ONE TWO THREE

1- The face of the poor little girl in the tenement yard in Glasgow 1971
2- The small dog on the side of the road
3- An arm all by itself near the train tracks
4- A monument to an unknown war hero
5- A mother with a carriage confused
6- An old tuberculosis hospital in ruins
7- The ocean a dead fish washed ashore
8- Outside the supermarket in the back the dumpster
9- The loser in a prize fight bloodied
10- Third grade 1956 Chicago 24 students in a row
11- Fire engines screaming down the street the tiller truck driver turns the corner.
12- Small boy the ice cream cone melting in the summer heat
13- Baseball stadium hot dog in a wrapper flying through the air
14- Rich man on his yacht bored
15- Car overheated on the side of the Interstate in Idaho 1969
16- The Bronx sometime in the past East 138th St
17- A farmer in his Farmall tractor planting Alfalfa
18- A world leader lying in state laying still in his coffin
19- A bed of roses it's raining
20- A muezzin calls the faithful 1922
21- 4 nuns get on the bus St. Louis
22- The surgeon begins to remove the tumor
23- Small girl in a shoe store they do not fit
24- The man turns to look behind realizes it is the last time
25- Somewhere in the universe

PLACE A COIN ON THE EYES

Place a coin on the eyes
For they see no more
Place a coin on the eyes
For your love to last evermore
The last memory
Of your loved ones face
Never to be hidden in this place
Place a coin on your loved ones eyes
Shadow of the memory
Reflection of the sky
Shed a tear let it drip to the ground
Silently so never a sound
Place a coin on the eyes of one now past
This world this life was never meant to last
All the life and love quiet now
So place a coin on the eyes to formalize the deal
In this moment there is no appeal
Stand in your Kirk or wherever you bow down
There is no key to open the ground
Place a coin on your loved ones eyes
Never again to see you
There is no surprise
Shed your tears release your fears
Close the eyes with a coin one last time
Place a gentle kiss
On their forehead
No one knows who is next in line

POETIC JUSTICE

I have been hauled into the court
The court of words
No one likes what I display
There are those who say
They smell like turds
Where is your poetic license they implore to spill this trash
There is a proposal to turn my words into ash
Yes, burn them along with the one who writes this trash
And has the nerve to misspell and have no punctuation
And thoughts are trite, show this reprobate a period or comma
We are sick of all his drama
The peasants are armed with pitchforks and gas
And stand outside the gates
Waiting for me to run into their arms
Oh, how they hate enjambment
I've done it again
And will continue much to their disdain
I have been given poetic license
By the powers that be and I shall remain
A thorn in their sides
Though even I do not write in iambic pentameter
Perhaps I should
I want to make it clear
I will not anyone else steer
My ship at sea for all to see
So much for that, I smell a rat
There are those who say I am a boudoir poet
My words only meant to seduce
If I am then I say let it produce
The beauties that lay before my feet
I would prefer to meet
Without any clothes
Perhaps I shall give up this poetic job
And write short stories with the same disregard
An entire novel with only one sentence
600 pages oh how novel that would be
I am going to let it be before they find me and
Hang me from a tree

CAVE CANEM

POMPEI

The tiles all fall together
Line up on the floor
The mosaic of the dog still stands guarding the door
Two millennium later after the violence of the gods
Our dog remains on guard on the floor.
Fidelis oh fidelis or Fido if you care
Guard my home and my love like you once did before
Our kisses fell like the tiles lined up in some cosmic trance
There is no one to record this our warm embracing dance
Herodotus is long gone he no longer looks at the sky
But our kisses like the tiles will endure for millennia as time passes by
And our faithful dog will stand guard over our hearts long gone
Oh fidelis oh fidelis or Fido if you care
You lay on the floor
Guard our home and our hearts like you once did before
The tiles all lined up like our kisses no more
Oh fidelis oh fidelis or Fido if you care
Guard our home and our hearts as you once did before
So long after the ashes fell
In the now quiet streets
The silence of Vulcan shows all is well
But our dog whose name is now lost in time
Still lays on the hearth
Guarding the door
The kisses of a husband and wife in joy are no more
No one knows of the love and pain of what passed before
Oh Fidelis oh fidelis or fido if you care
Guard our home and our hearts as you once did before
One day the violence will come anew
No one knows the time but the place is assured
And bury our dog for many millennium to come
And one day will be unearthed to show once more
The faithful dog guarding the door
Who will guard our home and our hearts as he once did before

Though I was the one
Who was dying inside
Seeing the tear stained face
Once was my bride

PRISON HEART

I could have held you so close and so tight
Your eyes glistening with tears in the waning light
You said I had beautiful eyes
Never saw that or said that before
You stood there in the grass tears streaming from your face
Never before never in that place
Where our love died more than once
I could have held you so close and so tight
That moment in time it all seemed so right
But the bars my prison heart could not defend
You never came to see me
From that place you would send me once again
You looked up to see me once more that last day
I thought you were my life
But that was another time
But the bars my prison heart could not defend
You were so alone
Though I was the one
Who was dying inside
Seeing the tear stained face
Once was my bride
But the bars my prison heart could not defend
I could have held you so close and so tight
Your eyes glistening with tears in the waning light
That moment in time it all seemed so right
You were so alone
Though I was the one who was dying inside
Seeing the tear stained face
Once was my bride

Musty smells of old dog
Is that death nearby or something else

PUT ON YOUR BOG SHOES AND WALK

Weathered barn red
How sad the hay rolls
Layed out on the field
Like an endless game of chess on the newly mown grass
Played out in some lifetime past
The silos now empty sentinels over the waving fields
Musty smells of old dog
Is that death nearby or something else
A lifetime passes
Only our possessions show a trace of what once was
Put on your bog shoes and walk boy
It is a long and lonely road
You have a great distance left to go
Once there was a girl yes so calm and sweet
Forget her now
She is only a signpost of the past
Put on your bog shoes and walk boy
There is a long road behind you
And a long one ahead

The clowns weren't too funny
The magician killed the bunny

READY

I am ready to die
Ready to go
Which way
I have no way
To know
Driving a stick
Driving to hell
Stuck in first gear
The going is slow
Stopped along the way
To watch the show
The clowns weren't too funny
The magician killed the bunny
Drank one too many shots
Slept it off in a skid row hotel
Woke up in a fog
Driving a stick
Driving to hell
Stuck in first gear
The going is slow
Dust rising from my tires
Leaving a trail
No one will follow
No one wants to fail
To tell me
I'm going the wrong way
Driving a stick
Driving to hell
Stuck in first gear
The going is slow
Ain't afraid of dying
I'm ready to go

ROGER WILCO

I send out your name in the night
Waiting for your reply
The radio is dead
Transmission is cut off
Roger Wilco Over and Out

Where are you in the firmament
Where are you in my dreams
Why don't you answer
No transmission
The radio is dead
Roger Wilco over and out

I scream out your name to the ether
I want you near
I type your name in code
But you don't hear
No transmission
The radio is dead
Roger Wilco over and out

There always was an answer
That is until now
You always sent your answer
No matter where you were
But no transmission
The radio is dead
Roger Wilco over and out

I thought I heard your call
But it was only static
Not you at all
No transmission
The radio is dead
Roger Wilco over and out

RUST

I saw your face in a dream
I didn't remember you ever smiling like that
It was a pleasant surprise
Hidden behind my eyes
The railings now all turned to rust
No hand hold before my trust
Left impressions in the sand
Shield my eyes from the flakes of rust
Knowing all will turn to dust
The old streets now memories
But somehow changed
No hand hold evermore
No foot hold beneath the floor
Plant my feet upon the ground
The sand now slides
Into the well
As I fall within
My hand does rise
To grab the railing
But much to my surprise
All has turned to rust
Before my eyes
Even the bricks and stones
In the foundation wall
No longer support
Anything above at all
The windows now all boarded up
No prying eyes to peer beyond
As I slide down within my dream
I thought I knew these streets so well
Not the portal to my private hell
I saw your eyes
Without a tear
Before the railings
All turned to rust

SHARDS OF POTTERY

All the kings and queens
Shards of pottery remain
Nothing left of the memory
Of their reign
All the poor unwashed and hungry
In the same refrain
Like shards of pottery
All that will remain
No one notices or for that matter cares
Time the eternal washer
Wipes away the stain
For you who screams out to heaven
For the memory to be preserved
When you are forgotten
Do not be perturbed
All the kings and queens you worshiped
The boat long gone has sunk beneath the sea
Like shards of pottery
A memory of what once was
And your place in eternity

Knowing full well at exactly that time
I too stare at the very same star
And we send our love from wherever we are

SHARE

All these moments
That we share
In what way can we care
To show each other
The feelings deep within
A simple touch
Can mean so much
Far more than a thousand words
A casual look from over the book
As we read from the peace within
Take my hand
And walk by my side
As I walk beside you
There is nothing to hide
The river is deep and wide
As it flows to the sea
Carrying our love
As it was meant to be
Silently there is no storm
Reminding us while we are apart
That love flows quietly
As it courses through our veins
Each night no matter how far away we are
Look to the sky and stare at the star
Knowing full well at exactly that time
I too stare at the very same star
And we send our love from wherever we are

Can you free me
Before I slide beneath the waves

SLIDE BENEATH THE WAVES

How can I reach you
How may I teach you
Before I slide beneath the waves
Can you see me
Can you free me
Before I slide beneath the waves
When was the last time we spoke
Was it before we awoke
In some distant memory
Of tear stained smoke
Was it before we sank beneath the waves
In which house do we reside
In what way does our love abide
Tell me now
Tell me how
Before we slide beneath the waves
No way to ignore
The tears that fall
To the floor
In what house did we reside
The stars as they shift
Will decide
In which direction we can hide
Before we slide beneath the waves

SORRY I MADE YOU CRY

Sorry I made you cry
I didn't even try
To wipe away the tears
Wash away all your fears
Even my words
Fell on deaf ears
I didn't think
I could reach into your soul
Reveal all the pain
You had hidden so well
Didn't think I could tell
Where truth and lies collide
Lay by my side
There is nowhere to hide
I won't hurt you again
Tears run down your face
There is no other place
Not in this time and space
Sorry I made you cry
I didn't even try
To wipe away all the tears
Calm all your fears
Sorry I made you cry
I didn't even try
To wipe away all your tears.

Every great blaze starts
With but a tiny spark into the tinder

THE FLAME CASTS NO SHADOW

The flame casts no shadow
As if you didn't know
You never know it's behind you
Its shadow does not show
A shadow is the absence of light
The flame blazing bright
Erases the shadow in the night
I wish to hell I had been there to guide you
I tried to tell you once before
The ocean has no shadow
No bottom and no floor
The flame can only guide you in the absence of light
Just because it's true doesn't make it right
Take from me all you can see
Let me be your guiding light
Pull you from the roiling waves
Just once more in the darkest night
The flame casts no shadow
How can you not fail to see
I never thought for a moment
That you would cease to be
Forever to hold you in my dreams
Deep into eternity
This flame we speak of
The one that flamed once bright
Was only tinder
Flickered and went out
It had no shadow to see it cast
No fuel to make it last
Every great blaze starts
With but a tiny spark into the tinder
We never know how much warmth it will throw
Or when the flame will burn low
But as always the flame has no shadow
And as such no direction to show.
The candle that burns the brightest
Is always the first to go
The flame in its incandescence
Illuminates with its glow
The warmth it leaves
Stays with all that know
The flame has no shadow
As if you did not know

THE GOOD THIEF

The good thief
No one knows your name
Perhaps you were saved
When you were made to pay
Your confession paved the way
For your soul that day
Please remember me
When I arrive at your gate
Remember me for no one else will
I was on your right
And asked to reman by your side
You were scourged 39 times
I felt your pain
As I looked into your face
That time so long ago
In a foreign place
Who was on the hill to watch us
Who bowed down in shame
Were you their savior
Savior to the lame
What were you thinking
Hanging next to me
Your final touch with humanity
A common thief in praise of thee
One more thief on your other side
A reminder of the trinity
Another soldier threw the spear
The final indignity
My legs were broken
Before the words were spoken
Before I appeared in front of you
On that day
One good thief
I remain

Only vibrations left in time
Reverberate and amplify

THE LAW OF UNINTENDED CONSEQUENCE

The Titanic is long gone
Sank beneath the waves
The bullet left the Fabrique National
Did its damage
Long ago
Each moment
No one sees
No one to believe
What mortals conceive
The blood left on the carriage
Led to the carnage
Untold misery
For a century or more
Each ill conceived notion
Part of the potion
That minds conjure
The law of unintended consequence
No recompense
For good or evil deeds
Only vibrations left in time
Reverberate and amplify
As the ricochet hits
One more target
An endless cycle
To begin again
A geometric progression
From drops to gallons to oceans
Of misery
One tiny piece of lead
Slides down the barrel
One wrong turn
One outstretched arm
One Archduke
One viral particle
One cosmic ray
One altered DNA
The law of unintended consequences
Pave the way

THE MIST IN MY EYES

The mist in my eyes
Makes me realize
All time passes
Until now
What is the link
That makes me think
I could have changed anything
With my thoughts
Engraved in time
The lessons were never so sublime
So that I could not see
What was never meant to be
I always thought
That life was forged
On the anvil of pain
The hammer blows
For those that chose
To stand in shame
For all to see
But never to be
One with their name
It was always the same
As before
Now you look and see
What others can be
Though they too
See through
The mist in their eyes
But also never realize
The cords that tie
Us together
All as one
Never come undone

Get down on your knees
Whisper to the ants
Show me if you please

THERE'S A CRACK IN THE SIDEWALK

There's a crack in the sidewalk
Why don't you take a look
Perhaps even better than reading a book
There's a crack in the sidewalk
Get down on your knees
Whisper to the ants
Show me if you please
Take me on a journey
To antland and beyond
Introduce me to your queen
And show me your realm
Look even closer
There's a wealth to behold
Put on your glasses
There's a story to be told
There once was a king
In the days of old
He was afraid of cracks
So he had them all sealed
He was afraid of falling in
And being swallowed up
So he never did look within
And see the wonders there
Don't make the same mistake
There is so much to take
From a simple crack within
The world is in your grasp
Grab it while you can
You will never regret
Bowing down on your knees
Seeking the knowledge if you please
Within a crack
There's a crack in this world
With knowledge inside
And within this crack
Nothing can hide

The dogs ran astray
In the ruins

THERE WAS SOMETHING LEFT UNSAID

There was something left unsaid
In the time of dread
Whoever heard the speech
There was no one to reach
For the gun
The words did not flow
How was anyone to know
In just what order
In just what show
There was no one left to go
The way
No authority to pay
The tax or the toll
As the bell rung
The children in the chorus sang
Out of tune
The dogs ran astray
In the ruins
The noise was deafening
No one to hear the exact words
But everyone knew
There was something left unsaid
The actors gave their final bow
As they left the stage
The audience in a rage
Wanted to turn the page
On all that was said
But even then
There was a sense of dread
The words left unsaid

THEY SELL DREAMS

What do they sell there daddy?
They sell dreams
To all the lonely people who pass by
Why do they sell dreams
The people have none of their own
What do they wrap them in
They wrap them in thoughts
That others have left behind
How much does a dream cost
More than nothing
But less than something
Left out on the street corner
Named despair
Do all the stores sell the same dreams daddy
No some sell dreams woven of gossamer
Others sell dreams of desire
And yet others sell dreams of long lost love
Can we go into a dream store
You are too young
Your dreams are still within you
You can only buy dreams if you have lost yours
Who makes the dreams daddy
Lost souls who have never learned how to have ones of their own'
They weave them out of old tales they heard long ago
One day will I have to buy dreams
No not if you treasure yours and nourish them
And feed them with love
You will always have your dreams
For a very very long time
Good Night son
I love you

THOSE WHO LOVE

There are those who are weak
And those who are strong
Those who are right
And those who are wrong
As I write these words
Please help me differentiate
Between those who love
And those who hate
There comes a time in life
When we must make the choice
When it is to raise our voice
There are many times where
Quiet speaks louder
But know the difference
Before you shout
There is nothing more powerful
Than the word
No weapon strong enough
To stop you
From being heard
There may come a time
Where you place a rock
In your sling
But know beforehand
That peace it will not bring
Only a temporary respite
And that only words
Will truly end the fight
There are words that heal
And ones that make you feel
Connected to this place
That you kneel
So make your choice
There are those that love
And those that hate

THREAD

Each moment in time
Our thread is woven
Into the tapestry of life
All the moments
From our birth to our death
Woven tightly
At a point look how thin
Stretched almost to breaking
You almost died
But you survived
The thread now stronger
As it passes over all those threads
Of whom you've touched
Some run parallel
Never to meet
So close so near
Others are wound tightly
Until one ends
Time passes on this amazing tapestry
To be revealed in all its glory
Perhaps at the end of time
Mistakes immutable
Woven forever
The moments that we meet
The sad goodbyes
The first kiss
As we close the eyes
Never revealed
But woven in time
A record of life
Yours and mine

Three Sacred Words

Three sacred words
I long for your touch
Three sacred words
Can mean so very much
Three sacred words
Can scare you away
They are the same ones that will make you stay
Three sacred words can the deepest of wounds heal
They are the very same ones that will make. you feel
These words screamed out in the dark
Will somehow find you
When we are apart
Three sacred words are all that I have
They are my nutrient
They are my salve
These words can wound or save
It is your choice
And how you rejoice
When can I hold you close
And whisper them in your ear
Feel our hearts beat together
There's nothing to fear
These three sacred words
You know what they are
They have been whispered
Throughout time both near and far
When may I hold you close
And whisper them in your ear
Our hearts beating together
There's nothing to fear

Somewhere in our vision
The mistake of our decisions
Rises like an angry sea

TOMORROW NEVER COMES

I'll make love to you
Tomorrow
Never comes
All the moments in between
My vision sees into the past
The night it never does last
Try as we might
When dawn brings first light
The curtain comes down
On our dreams.
All those memories
Lost in time
Every day is like yesterday
There is no life
And death does not exist
Within this realm
Who stands on the stormy deck
In the darkest night
Who holds the wheel
Who stands at the helm
Charts the course
Avoids the rocks and
The island of remorse
Comes crashing down
On our heads
Somewhere in our vision
The mistake of our decisions
Rises like an angry sea
Only then can we see
Through the waves
And we realize
We are slaves
To our emotions
And our place in time
I'll make love to you
Tomorrow
Never comes

WE'RE GONNA DIE IN THE MORNING

Sorry no one informed you
Sorry to ruin your night
We're all gonna die in the morning
No use taking flight
There's no getting out of this one
No one cares about your plight
It's nothing you've done wrong
Nothing you've done right
Just the way the cards fall
The dice rolled the wrong way
Your time is up
Sorry the clock just ran out
Don't take it personally
Just the way things are
We're all gonna die in the morning
Breathe in and take your last breath
It really isn't so bad
No paying the car loan
Or the rent
Don't know where you're going
Perhaps heaven sent
Say goodbye to whoever
Make peace with whatever god you revere
No demon or saint to guide you
From this place you hold dear
We're all gonna die in the morning
Really nothing to fear
Don't pack a bag
You're not gonna need it
Just close your eyes and accept it
You're going on a trip
One way ticket
Really nothing to fear

The man with no brain
Is feeling no pain
The man with no love fits like a glove
The one with no arms and legs
Is a master with pegs

THE FREAK SHOW

Welcome to the freak show where everyone knows
And everyone shows what liars propose
Where no one goes against the grain
There is no pain for those that remain
In their seats a spectacle
Resolves to be shown to all those unknown
Since the beginning of time
The audience cheers awakening their fears
Not to be like the ones onstage
Throughout every age while turning the page
Of the program the man with no brain
Is feeling no pain
The man with no love fits like a glove
The one with no arms and legs
Is a master with pegs
Which he fits in the holes that everyone knows
Are neither round nor square, the limelight burns bright
Illuminating the fright chased into the night
By the very real plight
Of all those who dare
To stop and stare
At the stage in their lives
When nothing is won under the sun
Under the tent where lifetimes are spent
The freak show begins
All welcome to come in
The freak show begins

WELL-ROTTED MANURE

No stick no stones no broken bits of glass
and no fire fanged manure
Only fresh manure horse or cow
no less than six months old
So that is the gestation period the quickening the heartbeat already felt
Three more months and a baby pops out of the womb
No sticks no stones no broken bits of glass
and no fire fanged manure
Turned well and no sawdust at all
How long before the pile of shit is ready to spread on your field
your flowers your vegetable garden
A new life springs forth from the organic waste
of our bovine and equine friends
But I digress no sticks no stones no broken bits of glass
no fire fanged manure and certainly no sawdust
Not in my mix not in my grandmother's recipe for borscht
She came here already broken from Europe and the Tsars horsemen
I bet Nikolai did not have sticks or stones
or broken bits of glass mixed in with his royal manure
His royal pile of shit an empire broken in bits
Waiting for act two to take place too
bad he would not live to see it along with the rest of his tragic family
My train takes me past the desolation of our landscape
the factories now gone only the chimneys remain
A mute testimony Our greatness lies in ruins
So, I scream out to the bent bricks what did you once make
and the chimneys answer
Smoke we made smoke
I say no the broken bricks scattered at my feet
once the bloody mortar held together
What the fuck did you make and the answer comes back even louder
We made smoke
Why do I even bother to look amongst the empty bottles
the bricks the empty buildings and
apartment torn curtains fluttering in the wind the broken windows
screaming at me look at our tears
look at our blood look at our desires flushed down the drain
along with our dreams
Who the hell are you to ask?
You know the answer already
No sticks no stones no broken bits of glass
and no fire fanged manure

WHEN WAS THE FIRST TIME

When was the first time I knew you were drifting away
Sliding towards the corner of oblivion in my life
When did I realize the warm kisses were no longer real
One more time
I knew
When the first moment came
Crashing down
And lay at my feet
I tried to make believe I did not see
What I knew
It doesn't matter anymore
The words stuck on my tongue like glue
And I could not shake them free
One last time
To tell you
To hold you
One last time
When was the first time I knew it was the last time
To even see you
In my time of my life
It doesn't matter anymore
It has all happened before
It doesn't make it any easier to say goodbye
To close the book
To take one last look
There is no one to blame
There is no time for shame
When it is the last time
To say goodbye

WHERE ARE YOU HIDING

I can feel you near me
You have always been there
But I can't see you
Where are you hiding
I want you near me
I turned around in the dark
There was no sound, you were just out of reach
What were you trying to teach me pain
There was no game I played
There was no time I waited in the rain
For you to brush up against me and say my name
Where are you hiding
I can feel you near me once again
I've never seen your face
But I would know you any place
You may be
For I can see the space
In between the lines
Wherever you may hide
I can feel you near me
You have always been there
Just out of reach
I can smell your perfume intoxicating me as I close my eyes
But when I open them I can't see you
Where are you hiding?
I want you near me
Do not fear me
I long for your touch I've never known
Only in a dream
But so it does seem
So real
I can feel your breath on my neck
I can feel you near me
You have always been there
But I can't see you
Where are you hiding?

WHO ARE YOU

Who are you
I said to the dark
A voice came back
Shortly
And who are you
To have such a request
I was just taking
A walk in the park
And wanted to know
Who possesses the dark
I don't usually answer
Mere mortals
Came the reply
In order to truly understand
It is essential to die
With a touch of bravado
I challenged the voice
I stand before you
Why don't you just try
And separate me
From my mortal coil
Or is this just some kind of joke
And I am just your foil
Arrogant little git aren't you
To challenge the dark
I will make you run screaming
From this very same park
Looking at my watch
I cleared my throat
And fairly shouted
It's you that is living on borrowed time
It's almost dawn
And the light is mine
Slowly but surely
Across the horizon
There was a thin red line
As I walked through the park
The morning was divine

"The heat between our bodies
The friction in our souls
Could melt steel"

WISH I COULD HOLD YOU

I made love to you as if in a dream
You lay there with your eyes closed
Naked before me
Your lips wet with desire
Ignites the fire
That burns within our loins
The words we whisper
In each others ear
That no one else can hear
Please let me in
To your sacred place
The passion of our embrace
Reveals upon your face
The deep desire within
I wish I could hold you
Like this forever
Naked as we were born
The heat between our bodies
the friction between our souls
could melt steel
All the moments
That we feel
The passion flows like a river
Between our legs
Entwined
Please let this last
A feast repast
The point is reached
Of release
We fell on each other
As we were spent
No time to repent
No reason not to start
Once again
Our lips locked together
Joined at our hips
Two became one
As bright as the sun
Till our passion was done

YOU COULD HAVE BEEN PRETTY

The lines worn in your face by time
The shifting sands the child born
No love lost nothing gained
For you to cry
No reason left to wonder why
Elephants and jewels untold wealth
Walked where you stood
Forlorn with child born
Perhaps of love
The stars were all ablaze
That quiet winter night
Had I not caught you
Within my sight
Starlight starbright may I have the wish
I wish tonight
Somewhere warm to rest my head
Some one strong to ease my dread
Some place safe to place a child in their bed
When I looked in your eyes
The tears long gone
You forgot how to cry
You could have been pretty
Once long ago
A home coming queen
Perhaps in a dream
You could have been pretty
Now no one will know
The eyes with no tears
Nothing to show

YOU NEVER DANCED WITH ME

You never danced with me
You never really took a chance with me
Somewhere in Firenza
A joyous wedding took place
The music the dancing expressed the joy
We stood in the street outside the wedding feast
I took your hand and asked you for this dance
You turned away without giving me a chance
As years went by
I never asked you again
I can move now
I can move now
In the light
In the day time
In the night
You never danced with me
You never really took a chance with me
You never saw me move
I could have swept you away
You never wanted to stay
From that day on
You never danced with me
You never really took a chance with me
I can move now
I can move now
In the light
In the daytime
In the night
You never danced with me

YOU SAW

You saw the veins on my arms
And like every Junkie
Thought of where you could hit
That would take away the pain in your life
As you ran your hands on my chest
Lay your head to rest
Within my arms
The hunger came
back once again
Needing to be fed
Sneak away one more day
One more time, buy one more dime
Bag of junk
Think I didn't know just where you did go
A little excursion to the other side of town
Think no one would see
What you tried to hide from me?
Plain as the map on your arms
Like highways all colored in blue
You sold your body and your soul
All for dreams that you could not realize
I saw it in your eyes
Before all the Lies
Fell from your tongue
But like every Junkie
There was always one last hit
Before the final note was played

It really didn't matter
Who you held that night
Whiskey wisdom
Would guide you to the light

YOU WALK IN YOUR OWN FOOTSTEPS

You walk in your own footsteps
You hide in your own shadow
You always turn the same corner
Before time catches you looking back
At the time you once knew
Before you were one
With yourself
How in the hell
Did you find yourself
Once you were lost
How did you lose yourself
And at what cost
You more than a days wage
Before you realized
It was too late to turn
The page
Never once did you waver
As you placed your bet
You tore up the ticket
And lit a cigarette
Smiled at the pretty girls
Who all passed you by
After all who would look back
At a man with one eye
To the future
And one to look behind
As you always knew
All you had to do was
Turn on a dime take one step to
The left or right
It really didn't matter
Who you held that night
Whiskey wisdom
Would guide you to the light
You walk in your own footsteps
And hide in your own shadow
As you walk through the night

Your hair upon the pillow
The strands you left
Mark our time
In this life

YOUR SOFT BREATH

As I fall into the void
Your soft breath upon my chest
Tells me you are safe
Within my arms
You have no qualms
To release your fears
Dry your tears
I miss that so
I let you know
Your hair upon the pillow
The strands you left
Mark our time
In this life
I long for your touch
Your lips on mine
Will I ever see
That time again
I long for your hand
Intermingled with mine
A moment in time
Standing on the tower Eifel
The lights of Paris
Spread out below
Two became one
Within the glow
I did not know
How precious those moments could be
I long for your lips
Softly on mine
I long for your voice
Measure of time
I long for your hand
Intermingled with mine

No matter the distance
That we walked alone
You were always by my side
As I was by yours

IN ANOTHER TIME

In another time
In another universe
We would have met
When we were young
We had no idea
Who we were
We could not see any further
Than our eyes could tell
The truth always matters
To all the saints and sinners
We met along the way
No matter the distance
That we walked alone
You were always by my side
As I was by yours
Walk in lockstep
But always alone
The vibrations of the Universe
Always rang loud
In our ears
Erase all the fears
And all the tears
Shed along the way
In another time
In another universe
We would have met
When we were young
The time has come
To pull aside the curtain
Of this I am certain
Turn back the clock
And never look back
In another time
We would have met
When we were young

Let me come into your arms
And hold me tight
As you did before
Never let me go
Never let me know
If you stop loving me

HOLD ME ALL THROUGH THE NIGHT

Hold me all through the night
Let me come into your arms
And hold me tight
As you did before
Never let me go
Never let me know
If you stop loving me
I will shine the light of my love
In your eyes
And make you realize
I will always be by your side
Hold me all through the night
Let me come into your arms
And hold me tight
As you did before
Our bodies fit just right
Your soft breath on my neck
Tells me I can close my eyes
Feel your heart beating
Next to mine
We always align
No how far away
Either of us may stray
I will always be next to you
As you are to me
Hold me all through the night
Let me come into your arms
And hold me tight
As you did before

ABOUT THE AUTHOR

Rick Savage (Richard) was born in Manhattan, New York, in a year well before now. He was supposed to be a doctor, but life took him in other directions. He has been a cinematographer, director of special effects, engineer, and poet. He pleads the Fifth on anything else you may have heard.

When asked, Rick's daughter and friends offered the following insight. Generous, industrious, persevering, tough as shit, New Yorker, the genuine article.

—Haley Jane Savage

Steadfast, generous, and always ready to help true blue mob couture.

—Marilyn Horan

A palm tree in an endless cyclone. Bending not yielding. He never tires of overturning flat rocks and rotted trunks, thrilling at discovery. So he is a poet now? I thought he was still working at the Pachyderm club. Sirens welcome his approach. Lobsters lament. Whatever has not killed him, tried really hard.

—J Del Rossi. 21

I am not sure that I would want a complete dossier on my own father, Rick, and while I can't say for certain if he's ever run guns, I can tell you I'd bet on 22 at his roulette table. But Dad, in my preferred parlance, is more than the sum of parts and references. I would say he is the fabric of the City—he is a carbon arc, he is Luna Park, he is a span of steel across the river and against the sky—but his city is a dream and the spirit of the stories for which he is a vessel pre-date Peter Minuit. The lamp he lifts will show you where you need to go. Good luck.

—Matt Savage

Resilient.Brilliant,Softhearted.Incomparable gearhead. And like all good poets ,a bit egocentric...in the nicest way possible

—Laura Harris

www.ingramcontent.com/pod-product-compliance
Lightning Source LLC
Chambersburg PA
CBHW060757100426
42813CB00004B/860